T0156944

DIFFERENT SHADES OF GREY

Alex van der Mout

iUniverse, Inc.
New York   Bloomington

Different shades of grey

This is a work of fiction. All of the characters, names, incidents,
organizations, and dialogue in this novel are either the products
of the author's imagination or are used fictitiously.

iUniverse books may be ordered through booksellers or by contacting:

iUniverse
1663 Liberty Drive
Bloomington, IN 47403
www.iuniverse.com
1-800-Authors (1-800-288-4677)

Because of the dynamic nature of the Internet, any Web addresses or
links contained in this book may have changed since publication and
may no longer be valid. The views expressed in this work are solely those
of the author and do not necessarily reflect the views of the publisher,
and the publisher hereby disclaims any responsibility for them.

ISBN: 978-1-4502-4491-6 (pbk)
ISBN: 978-1-4502-4492-3 (ebk)

Printed in the United States of America

iUniverse rev. date: 7/9/2010

There are many who have helped me on this journey to become the person that I am. To all my friends (Logan, Alain, Sophie, Chanel and many others), family and colleagues, thank you for your belief in me. A special thanks and dedication goes to Dan Paradis, who through his guidance has made me a better person. Out of the mist you have touched my world; I know not where I would be without you. Thank you so very much.

When asked "Why do you do what you do,
Why write poetry?"
Softly I replied
"I'm finally able to put words to my emotions."

January 12, 2010

They are soldiers
Fighting a fight of survival
The battlefields are their homes
Blasted apart by no weapon;
They are at war, with things they built
The dead aren't unknown
The blood of children, brothers, mothers
Is more accessible then water
Bodies litter the streets where children once played
They are soldiers

Shed a tear O'Earth
Feel the horror, the terror
See the pain in their haunted eyes
Hear their desperate pleas!
See the destruction
Help you mighty ones!
How the misfortunate need your help!

Haiti, we are here

Never able to die

If I were to die tomorrow
What would the world say of this vessel of dust?
When these pages fade and crumble
What essence is left behind?
A few would weep, but tears will dry up.
Crisp memories will fade to a haze
But a dark memory, hidden
My body would rot and become one with the earth.
But I would not be dead, let me live, if you will
When I fall, read my soul, see what you have missed
No emotions I showed; to the world I poured them out
Read the fire on these pages, let it light up the darkness
On these pages my life is written
When you read, I can never die.

Chapter One

Everyone has a story, mine is still in chapter one
I write these words to escape this conflict
A refugee of this world
Letters one after another, words after words
When the sword makes first contact
The paper trembles at the message it is to proclaim
Sentences form, emotions flow
Lies don't shape words
These letters spell truth, believe
They play a melody known to me alone
When I'm gone these words won't be
They will spell the paragraphs of my live
Merging, flowing, joining together
A story, a journey
Of love, that'll make your heart ache
Of sadness, tears will run away
Of anger and rage, volcanoes erupting
Of anguish, if only you knew
A struggle within, forcing sides to be chosen
No author am I, a storyteller yes
Far better then I are to be found
Among the Great I am not to be found
The Great will read and scoff, disrespectful
Don't critic the patterns of words you cannot relate
These words won't see the far ends of the earth

Impartial men will read and not change
Wars will not come to a halt
Who will see the fire burning these pages?
A few will read and let it burn
But, if YOU read
Read between the lines
And see ME, as I truly am
Then I am content
A story is powerful when one reads
Read! Release me from these chains
Let me live through you, once more let me live
Read with eyes that few have opened
From these pages to your world let me run
I'll show you the light
From light darkness is banished
No more shadows
A cove of truth lays bare
No more false fronts does he project
All is open
Let me live!
Read my soul, my story
Feel my pain, my love
Know me, the secret life I live
For in day I walk, shrouded in darkness
How little the world sees

Squeeze

Squeeze the butterfly in your hand
Where is it to go?
But seep through your veins

Life

With eyes of contempt
She gazed at the sea of mankind
Their turbulent nature
Their lust for hate
Over shadows their ability to reason and to love
Curious creatures these men
Through fire they are forged
Yet a breeze breaks them
What do they deserve?
What is to be the fate of this flighty creation?
Do I give destruction or sanctification?
To the test they are to be put
Every nightmare will become a reality
Some will break, some will become stronger
From the abyss their fears come hauntingly
"You take all the trash and all the gore,
HA HA
HERE! Have some more!"
Life, can really be a bitch

Our madness

1000 dead on one side
1000 more on the way to the grave
Land without meaning
Stained with the blood of the damned and innocent
As rain gently falls
Washing the crimson liquid to the depths of the earth
Clearing the land of sin
For the freedom of our lives
Our flag flies high
Telling the dead who the day has won
Telling the living the purpose of our madness
A hundred men will perish before the flag falls
For the flag is us
Fluttering in the wind, yearning to be set free

Who I am

I am
Past, present, future
I am
Now and for all eternity
I see all
Yet know nothing
Time is but a shadow
Forever stalking me
The memories of the past haunt me
Feelings and emotions
None that I have experienced
I see, I feel
Such terrible pain
Of men killed in battle
His woman mourning his death
It means nothing,
The affairs of men
Are none of my concern
For I am the immortal guardian
While they perish
I live

The Tree and the Rose

Good things come in small sizes
Beauty minimized to absolute perfection
How could a lofty tree love such perfection?
When one bends the maple to the height of the rose
Anything is possible

Home

My stronghold
Has crumbled
They mobilize their attack
I can't keep them back
So I hide
In myself
My home
Has become
A battlefield

Problems of Today

With the wave of her hand
She brought death to the land
Misery and gloom
Filled the earth with doom
Told not to look
But a peek was all it took
Before she closed the lid
Hope fled

Expression

Poetry written in the heart
Never fully expressed by the word

The Tapestry

The stones are damp
Water drips in the distance
The storm rages on
But the mighty castle will not yield

As sleep eludes him
The heir of the ancestral house:
The duke to be
Creeps down to the lower levels

Eyes linger on the great tapestry
A scene of a great battle
The battle that dwarfed all battles
Where a hero emerged

With weary eyes
Closing to blissful slumber
The mind's eye opens
To a clash of swords

Punishment

The worst punishment of one
To erase their deeds from history
Their presence on this world
As nothing

Into the crimson night

I flee
I withdraw
I can't take the sounds
They're in my head
Screaming my name
Why won't they go away?
So I run
When I stop they catch up
So I keep running
Never stopping
The sun sets
The sounds get louder
I ran into the crimson night

Why Me?

I hate the way you don't approve
I hate that I can do no right
Everything I do is wrong
Nothing is right
I am nothing
Dear god, I pray
Why me?

Water

Water, giver of life
Redeemer of sins, quencher of fire
Poseidon, vast power in your grasp

Guilt

I am horrified by what I've done
So much blood on my hands
That not even the watery deeps
Can wash them clean
I have made fathers bury sons
And mothers weep for daughters
For what?
For an idea
An idea of serenity
A forced serenity
I thought I was doing good
But no amount of prayer
Can forgive me for what I've done
I ask for forgiveness
But none is deserved
I bare my chest
And ask you to take revenge
For blood shed is blood redeemed
But no one lifts a hand
Forcing me to face my guilt

The puppeteer

Bow before me!
All you worthless swine,
Kneel before your master
I own you!
You, you are nothing
I? I am all powerful
And wise
I know you
Even better than you know yourself
Many have tried to usurp me from my throne
HA! I scoff at their petty rebellions
I am the master puppeteer

Innocence Awaits

The noose is tied
The gallows are set
Awaits the condemned
Life and death hangs in the balance
An innocent man awaits his death
Five past the hour
The rope shall go taut
The gallows are set
The noose is tied

A Lost Soul

Why am I here?
What is my purpose?
Why are you here?
Here on this planet
No good have we done
All we have achieved is the death of our brothers
As a race what is our purpose?
God put us here for what reason?
What is expected of us?
What is a lost soul to do?

Hell on Earth

Those aren't just words, it is reality
The pain we've felt, the things we've seen
Evil all around, growing ever more
All feel the sweet kiss of this world
That death baring sweetness.
Taste it, let it flow through your body
Let it take its course
As you see that blinding light
You will see Hell on Earth

Two worlds

When two worlds collide
Only history knows of the carnage left behind
Crows gather
To eat the bloody scrapes
Choking down the taste of men's pollution

The Price for Freedom

Death draws closer;
With his head held high
Locks eyes with the emperor
Roars with defiance
"I die free!"
His body slumps to the ground
Blood staining sand crimson
The great Gladiator has perished

Faint memory

So many faces that I do not know
Whirling around and around
Laughing, cringing, crying
Then POOF! They wither and die
A faint memory left behind

Unknown

Mother, daughter, father, unborn child
I am all
And none

I push and shove
Nudging others
To unseen paths

I manipulate
I force
I do nothing

I am nothing
And everything
I am the unseen

I am history, raw power, time, fate, and future
I am all
And none

I am just a fragment of the imagination

Graveside

Tears run down my cheeks
No one sees
Why would they?
They're not here
Nor do they care
They never saw my pain
Only you did
Now you're gone
And I'm at your graveside

Hand in hand

Hand in hand we have conquered the land,
Peace, love, hope,
Nourished a parched ground,
Peace united a peoples,
Love made enemies brothers,
But our hope has kept them true.

Live for me

When all seems lost
When all joys in life are gone
Why choose life when you can't feel anything anymore?
Live not for today
Nor for tomorrow
Live for life itself
For when one will say "I do"
Live for the unknown
Joys yet not experienced
Live for the sake of living
Live for me

Light

The candle
In bitter triumph
Teaches us darkness

So lost

I am unsure
No longer knowing what I'm to do
Lost in the sea of our time
Tossed about, nothing to hold on to
What path is laid before me?
What road shall my feet trod?
The good and the bad blur together
Left and right, which is which?
My brain swirls around and around
I hate and yet I love
Or do I? I don't know
What am I to do?
So lost, so lost

A martyr's final hour

I am anonymous
No great deeds have I done
In the eyes of the great I am nothing
Who will remember me when I am no more?

This is my final hour
I have been tried and convicted
When the clock strikes noon
The axe shall fall

Feel no sorrow for me
Hate not those guilty of my blood
I die for what I believe is right
I will die free

I no longer feel the dampness of my cell
Preparing myself for the bliss of my long rest
With my head held high I shall march to my death
Praying someday that all will live free

The Swing

There once was a girl on a swing
Who swung all day and all night
Swinging to forget
Forget all the things that happened
When the war to end all wars came and went
Killing all save one
And so she swung
Trying to forget

Gone to Sleep

Crisp memories fade to nothing
Vision grows blurry
Speech gets slurred
The world turns black
As the cradle rocks
The baby falls into slumber

The Power of Death

Death
Brings misery
Causes eyes to redden and tears to come forth
Even the mightiest of men give way to the sorrow of death

Death
Brings change
Through death one man can change the world
In death martyrs are born

Death
Do not mourn those who pass into death
Rather rejoice over the deeds of a man's life
Remember his actions and learn from them

Through death man realizes his insignificance
Through death man knows he is nothing
No man can stand firm against death
We must all sacrifice ourselves to its power

The Battle

All being called to the war
Young and old take up arms
Both sides draw up
As missiles fly through the air
Thousands fall
Blood runs as freely as water

Pressures amount
The battle rages
Both sides have heroes
But heroes can die
The strong and the feeble die together
Reinforcements being called up

A war that the earth never will witness
No one observes the battle
No one sees the torment
Behind these gentle blue eyes
A battle in my mind

Unfathomable

Inside white washed buildings
Misery and gloom reside
Behind their smiles
Is pain beyond compare
Their smooth words
Betray the echoes of past screams
Perfect families
Huddle together and fear
None perceive the unfathomable
Because it is in a utopia that they live

The world notices

In death men don't speak
But their graves are louder than any sound
When one falls
The world takes notice
And bombs fly in response

So long, goodbye

With final breathes
All men come to an end
Thus so do I
Though not of natural means
I leave this place
This place that has been merciless
Feel sorrow
Feel regret
Feel foolish
For this is your doing
I did you no wrong
But you have hurt me so many times
So many times
So, so long and goodbye

Pressure

They're in my head
All around
Whispering in my ear
When I turn to face my imagination, they're gone
Whispering in my ear
All around
"Make it stop! Please!"
But they don't stop
I feel their hands crawling over my body
Dragging me to my doom
"Help! Please, somebody help............PLEASE!"
No one hears
Nobody ever hears
My soundless sobs fill the air
Why doesn't anyone help?
Getting closer
Soon it'll be all over
My sobbing stops
I've lost the will to even utter my pain
Where is my hero?
My knight in shiny armor?
My thoughts in disarray
As they push me over the edge

Light at night

Its creation gives glory
To the orb that lightens a darkened world
To it they give all their praise
Seeing its faithful servants
It shines its light down below
Lightening the path of the blind.
Without the moon
Ours souls would be filled with despair

Grasp

The eerie silence screams through the air
Forcing all to stop and stare
None can see it
It can only be felt
Out of the pit it came forth
Unleashed on that innocent world
The foolish tried to run
But its dark grasp is everywhere
They scream and scream
Until they too are silent

Gazing

As I gaze out to the starry heavens
My uncertainty shines bright
Brighter than any star
Yearning to be set free
To sour upon unimaginary heights
Yearning to break the mold
That has been cast for me

Society

Society:
Abstract, hard
to understand, created
by governments, to
bind their populace

The memory

The wounds never healed
So deep they were
Caused not by weapons
But thoughts and looks
So despised I was

I never forgot
I remember the looks
I remember the cruel grins of success
After I'm lying in my own blood
I never forgot

Remember now you do?
As you grovel
Before me
So sorry you say you were
Who's bigger now?

May you never forget
You won't
I'll make sure of that
Why?
Because
I never forgot

Fight

I fight and I fight
Doing good, upholding the right
 I strike down the evil one
Those doing crimes for fun
I own the night
Doing evil until first light
When light shines upon my deeds
Into the shadows I flee

The Victory

A man's mark is left
On history itself
When his blood stains the ground
Through death the victory is won

Vacant Memory

Four bare walls
One door, bed, mirror
Nothing more
The locked door opens to nothing
The lumpy bed, no comfort
The mirror
In the mirror I see a face
That should be mine, but isn't
The face, lean, scarred, gaunt eyes
Not the handsome, unblemished face that used to stare back
How could this happen to me?
What have I done?
Don't know who I am or where I am
Panic surrounds me
What is going to happen to me?
Huddled in the corner
Trying to think
I remember the pain: Terrible pain
Pain from what?
Memories of what?
My vacant memory holds no answers
Perhaps one day
One day my memories may return and give me their answers
Until then
My eyes slowly close to a restless sleep

Running

Running, long strides measuring yards
Freedom is near, a light up ahead
Bullets leap through the air
Striking low
Eating away the flesh into moist innards
As life seeps away
Raises his middle finger in the age-old salute
Crumples to the ground
The light shines forth
Hiding his body amidst shadows

Horror

Guilt hangs over men's heads
Hunched over with the pain of the past
Only humans carry the horrors of yesterday, forever
It is our blessing
It is our curse

Drip Drip

Drip, Drip
Blood of my life
Gashed out by a knife

Drip, Drip
Falls to the ground
Forming puddles all around

Drip, Drip
I fall to my knees
To my name no good deeds

Drip, Drip
I fall and die
And in my blood I lie

Untitled

I went to war
To maintain the peace
Only to be buried in that foreign land

Outlook

My outlook was once bright
A different shade it has become
This transformation frightens me
Excites me, scares me, turns me inside out
This ain't paradise, this I know
This isn't punishment
It is simply me
Burning out of existence
But from the ashes I shall rise
With a fire in my eye, engulfing my soul
I will be forged into someone new
Ready to take on this forsaken land.

Opinion

Have an opinion:
They call you judgmental.
Have one not:
They call you a coward,
So I simply don't care

Ideology

Books of peace and prayer
Become ideology of war

Chains of resentment

You tie me up with these chains
Saying you'll protect me
Pull on them, the shorter they get
Protection from what?
Demons of the past, your experiences to the fore will come?
What evil will I see, what bad will tear me to pieces?
I pull on my chains, trying to learn in a complex world
I wish to see the free people
Yet, angry you get "how dare you yearn what is not yours!
As I have spoken you shall never escape."
Escape? I want the ability to see the world
The good, the bad, the undecided
These chains are my demons
Every fear linked together
Fear that they may tighten
These chains are the reason of my resentment!

Melody

There's a melody in the air
So beautiful, so deadly sweet
Ancient, yet new
Creation stands in awe
As the breeze envelops it
Winter turns to spring
Flowers erupt and join in this melody
So simple, as complicated as the universe itself
It is the creation of men
How we don't know what it is
Turn to your love
Create the melody that means so much
Say the frightening words
"I love you"
And see how the world can change

Emotion

Love is a fluid emotion
It is an ocean held at bay
Hidden, hard to find
Not to be found at a quick glance
Hand in hand
Cross that barrier
Let the torrent flow!

Saved and Killed

When I saw you
The fragments of my heart were glued
The broken halves were at once mended
But when your smile ended
And you continued on your way
My heart stopped beating that day

My love

Part 1
I see her from a distance
Standing so perfectly
No blemishes, no imperfections

I wish I knew her name
But know that none will truly capture her beauty
Standing there
Forcing me to ask

My love

Part 2
She is a dove
Among crows
Her beauty surpasses many
I know neither of her name nor her status in society
But I am content
To but gaze from a distance

My love

Part 3

A picture is worth a thousand words,
Then many will be needed.
To fully describe her in every aspect
Every freckle
Every lock of hair
Complete her
To describe her smile:
A gallery will be needed.
Because if perfection was such a thing
It would be her

This feeling

When our lips first touched
The person within was set free
The bars of rage and despair: dissolved
Me, the true me, emerged
No longer in darkness
I stepped into the light of your presence
You reached out
And lifted me from the depths of hell

This feeling II

I fell into this feeling
It is new, yet old
Old, as time itself
Happiness, joy, glee
Fill dark crevices in my mind
How to describe it?
Simply;
LOVE

One wish

If I had one wish
I would not wish for riches
Nor for glory
I would not wish for this pain to be taken away
For it has forged me into who I am
But, if I had one wish
I would wish for the two of us to become one
Forever

Once whole

Once whole
Now lays in two torn halves
Blood falls to the Earth
Rivers become oceans
The plight of one man against the world
Sends a message clear to the sky:
We were never meant to be alone

Angel

I think I saw an angel
Whose brilliance brightened an already lit room
Nothing is perfect; I disagree
Innocence in its pure form,
Walking among us

Missing

There's a piece of my heart missing
Pain fills my entire body
Blurs my vision, darkens my world
Nothing is the same again
Something is missing
I lost it when we parted ways

No air

Why don't I feel anything?
Because you numbed all my feelings
Took my breath away
And gave me no air to breathe

About a girl

With the spoken word,
My thoughts are not expressed
Give me the pen,
And I'll show you the depth of my soul
I am not able to say the words,
So allow me to spell it out.
Beautiful, Pretty, Cute
Are all singular words to describe you
I've been star struck every since I've meet you
When you are sad, I am pained
When you are joyful, I am happy
I do not know why
But when you're around
My world doesn't seem so dark
I think you already know all of this
But I think it best if I tell you
You are very special...to me
You are a beacon in a darkened world
Thank you, for letting me know you
I wish that we can expand on our friendship
And if you ever need anything
I will always be there for you.

Blackened Heart

I thought I was in love
So struck by Cupid's arrow
Awaiting everyday just to see your face
Now?
Now, I am filled with a burning rage
When I see you,
Holding hands,
With my former friend.

You

Your name tastes so sweet on my tongue
Your cool touch sends shivers down my spine
When I held you, life was good
Your presence
Illuminated the darkness of my void
But now you're gone
The coldness returned
Darkness unleashed
Consuming me alive

Faith

Row upon row
Blank faces alight with faith
Conjoining together, setting the room ablaze

Disrespect

You disrespect me momentarily with futile words of air
I will haunt you for eternity with words of ink

Mindless abandonment

So long ago, it seems
My dutiful guardians left
Leaving me in a vulnerable void
I have with-drawn into myself
So much I know not who I am
The hidden me, reaches out and these words form
The hollow body, only cuts himself
His mindless abandonment, grievous to all those around
I know not what I do at times
I can feel not the cost of my actions
Pain reaches through the haze, with it I grow
And deeper yet I hide
So many shields I have put up
No arrows, save one, has penetrated
After all, Cupid was always the best marksman

Truth

What is truth?
Truth is an ideal, perfect
People abuse it for their own ends
It is a life and death force
No one can see it
But all feel its crushing blow when it comes to a climax
Man strive for it, die for it
But truth cannot be held
For it is an idea, cannot be found
It is simply there
Beckoning
Laughing, when we fall of the edge

Creation of Men

In the beginning there was darkness
So dark that none could see
Filling the void of time
Misery and gloom

But there was hope
An orb of light lay suspended
A beautiful planet
Everything good, life

Darkness never to be outdone,
Created men

Ideal

What happens when you are brought up in an ideal,
a perfect ideal in every way,
what happens when the one you're supposed to respect and look
up to abuses the ideal?
Betrays everything you believe in?
Yet, only you know it
Others see a face, a new man he becomes to them, a man they
want to see
When he becomes the very demon you're fighting against
What happens?
You fight, actions and words contending
But yet no one notices, they only see his front and your
disrespect
What happens?
You begin to hate that one
You escape to friends, just escape
He disappears, as another takes his place
You begin to see truth as it really is
Truth can be hidden behind a false front
Break down the barrier, please
And see how dark my world can be

A boy with a stick

Lost in the maze with no walls
So lost, imaginary doorways appear
The stick in your hand becomes a mighty sword
The rags on your back become an impenetrable suit of armor
Boldly you go, not heeding your heart
When the dragon rushes
Realize
You are just a little boy with a stick
And just how lost you are

Here I stand

Pages from the good book
Form the path that I attempt to follow
So many distractions, leading to broken vows
I spin these words so you never find me
Hidden behind a mask of Shakespeare
Don't stand too close, the fire will burn you
I am what I set out to be
Friend, confident, savior and destroyer
A baby in the cradle
Half written verses, forgotten, yellowed with age
Who am I? What you make me.
Here I stand, facing down the barrel
Don't shoot, you are facing a mirror
Here I stand
Find me, living in a glass house
Here I stand, but waiting for you.

Journey

I'm on my knees
Not in submission, but begging for forgiveness
I'm a thousand miles away
Soon I'll make it to Jerusalem
In the wretched desert, let's find the oasis
Pray, it is not a mirage
Follow the rising sun
Let it be your beacon, when your world is at its darkest
Follow your heart, but also your mind
Let your journey guide and inspire others

Selfish

Is it selfish to wish the embrace of one whom you do not know?
Her beauty hurts your own soul
No blood falls to the ground
Gazes at you, but doesn't see you
Just another person in the background
Grant me courage, on my knees
I wish her to know my existence
How she haunts my life
Is it selfish, or just human?

Dream

Like Luther I have a dream
Not of unity but of purpose

I feel the way for my feet to trod
But they refuse to follow the beaten path

I'm a shooting star fleeing this darkened world
Help me find my resting place, and let me brighten your world

There's the smell of death in the air
My corpse falls to the ground; I walk away from this life

The questions in my head have no answers
Even if they did, who could interpret?

This dream never ends
No awakening there is for me

So vast my universe, it collapses in itself
My eyes open with a blinding blast of darkness

Solitude
(Co-author: Abigail van der Mout)

There's a certain beauty to fog
Concealing the sins of others
Reflecting our own

In solitude we walk
Thoughts swirling around us
Dissipating only when the sun rises

Final

The alphabet has run dry
No longer do words march at my command
Is my story over?
Will the world now cover over me,
to become but a footnote in a insignificant period of history?
I pray never may that be
My words will not be halted
Chapter one may be done
But the story never ends